James Hall

Price list of materials for painting on china

Firing and gilding for amateurs a specialty and at reduced rates

James Hall

Price list of materials for painting on china
Firing and gilding for amateurs a specialty and at reduced rates

ISBN/EAN: 9783337136567

Printed in Europe, USA, Canada, Australia, Japan

Cover: Foto ©Thomas Meinert / pixelio.de

More available books at **www.hansebooks.com**

ESTABLISHED 1873.

⇒ PRICE LIST ⇐

...OF...

Materials for Painting on China

Firing and Gilding for Amateurs

A SPECIALTY

AND AT REDUCED RATES.

CONTAINING ALSO

PRACTICAL INFORMATION

FOR

Painting on China, Gilding, Tinting,   ✳
   ✳   Groundlaying, Paste Raising, Jewel Work, etc.

JAMES F. HALL,

34 North Fifteenth Street,

PHILADELPHIA. PA.

September, 1897.

Eagle Printing House,
No. 13 North Thirteenth Street,
Philadelphia.

Introduction.

I BEG leave to thank my patrons for the kind favors they have bestowed on me for the last twenty-three years, both for their patronage and recommendation to their many friends, and I can assure them that I will do my utmost to give entire satisfaction in the future.

Allow me to present to you my newly revised Price List of materials for painting on China.

Since issuing my previous catalogue several new and useful colors, etc , have been placed on the market which I have added to this list.

I would like to call special attention to my new Matt and Enamel Colors for Tinting. These colors will be found very convenient, as they are ground as fine as it is possible to grind them, in oil ready for use. Directions will be found with list of colors.

Another new feature is my ready prepared Paste for Raised Gold and Enamels for Raised work, they require no extra grinding, are ready mixed with sufficient oil, and are worked merely with turpentine.

My Roman Gold and Bronzes are pronounced by all who have tested their value, to be equal to any and superior to many, both for quality, quantity and durability. See testimonials.

I have also added a full line of Mineral Decalcomania, with directions for transferring, etc.

I am pleased to mention that a reduction will be made on many of the articles, also in firing of several articles of china, while I shall always endeavor to have the quality to the highest standard.

All materials quoted in this Price List will be sent by mail, postage or expressage paid, except when otherwise stated.

All articles are packed with the utmost care and their safe delivery is guaranteed. Mail and express orders for Gold and Material will be shipped same day as received.

Remittances should be made by Bank Draft, Check, or P. O. Order For small amounts, less than one dollar, postage stamps will be accepted.

No charge will be made for packing.

All material will be shipped at my risk, and their safe delivery guaranteed.

Firing and gilding for amateurs a specialty.

I hold myself responsible for China that should happen to break in firing, but not in transit, although the greatest care will be taken in repacking.

Express and mail orders receive prompt attention, no extra charge for repacking.

Terms.—Strictly cash with order.

Yours respectfully,

JAMES F. HALL,

September, 1895.

HALL'S
Superior Roman Gold and Bronzes
FOR ROYAL WORCESTER and DOULTON DECORATIONS
ON CHINA OR GLASS.

PREPARED READY FOR USE IN BOXES OR IN GLASS JARS

Price, 75 Cents per 18 grain Box, Postage Paid.

ROMAN GOLD.
In Glass Jars, with Metal Air-Tight Lids, Postage Paid.

Two Box Jar,	containing same quantity as two boxes, price,		$1.50
Three "	" " " three " "		2.25
Four "	" " " four " "		3.00
Six "	" " " six " "		4.50
Eight "	" " " eight " "		6.00
Ten "	" " " ten " "		7.50
Twelve "	" " " twelve " ',		9.00

HARD GOLD FOR OVER COLORS
In Glass Jars, with Metal Air-Tight Lids, Postage Paid.

Two Box Jar,	containing same quantity as two boxes, price,		$1.50
Four " " "	" " " " four " "		3.00
Six " " "	" " " " six " "		4.50

Roman Gold in Powder, per dwt., ...75
Hard or Unfluxed Gold in powder, for over color, chemically pure
    per dwt 1.30

Roman Gold, for on white China and Paste and general use.
Hard or Unfluxed Gold, for over color exclusively.
Light Green Gold, for Vase Handles, Paste, Flower Work, etc.
Dark Green Gold, for Royal Worcester, Handles, etc.
Red Gold, for Royal Worcester Paste, Handles, etc.
Bronze Gold, for Handles, Vases, etc.
Dead Silver, for Royal Worcester, etc. 30 cents per box.
Dead Silver, in Powder. 25 cents per bottle.
Liquid Bright Gold. 75 cents per bottle.
Liquid Bright Silver. 60 cents per bottle.
Essence to use with Bright Gold and Silver, per bottle, 10 cents.

Roman Gold will stand on delicate tints of color (providing the color
has been first fired) and will prove as satisfactory as though Hard Gold had
been used; but for over medium and thick grounds, Hard Gold must be
used.

HOW TO APPLY AND MIX
Roman Gold and Bronzes.

If the Gold is needed for outlining, edges, or soliding handles, etc add a few drops of spirits of turpentine and mix thoroughly and thin enough to flow from the brush.   When the Gold on the glass slab becomes too dry or hard, that it will not mix readily with turpentine, add a drop or two of Bright Gold essence, heat the slab slightly, by holding it over a spirit lamp, or lighted match for a few seconds, and mix until glass slab becomes cold, adding turpentine while mixing until thin enough for working.   In applying the gold to china, cover the ware with a thin, but even coating, putting on a thick coat is of no benefit, as it is opaque and the surface only is seen.   It must be no wash however but a solid, even coat.   As the turpentine evaporates quickly, from the gold in working, a little should be added frequenty, and the gold remixed, the brush also requires frequent dipping in turpentine to keep the hairs all free and open.   For stippling use the gold very stiff, and never dip the stippler in turpentine, as it takes up too much, and makes the gold too thin.   Use brushes that have never been used for colors and keep a special slab or palette for gold to prevent waste from cleaning.   Roman Gold is for use on all plain china and for covering Paste for Raised Gold.   For over color use Harb or Unfluxed Gold only. Dead Silver and Gold Bronzes are mixed and applied in the same manner as Roman Gold.   After the Gold and Bronzes have been fired they may be either polished with the glass brush or burnishing sand.   If a very bright effect is desired, the gold should be burnished with a burnishing stone.   For engraving on the gold use an agate tracer.

A few extracts from letters and some

TESTIMONIALS

From a few of those using HALL'S ROMAN GOLD.

Wilkesbarre, Pa., Aug. 26, 1897.

James F. Hall, Philadelphia, Pa.:

Dear Sir: After eight years' experience in the use of gold for china decorating, during which time I have tried and used numerous preparations of gold for that purpose, I find that prepared by you to give me the most satisfaction. For brilliancy, color and richness of effect, I have never found it surpassed. While I do not dictate to my pupils what gold they shall use I have never hesitated about recommending yours to them. They also recognize its superior quality and are at present without an exception using it in their work. Sincerely yours, CHARLES WALLACE QUICKSELL.

Shenandoah, Pa., Aug. 21, 1897.

Mr. James F. Hall, Philadelphia, Pa.:

Dear Sir: It gives me great pleasure to recommend your Gold for china. I have always found it most satisfactory in its results. In short, I consider it perfect, and would not use any other. You are at perfect liberty to publish this statement. Miss Myra Hunt, "Yorkville," Pottstown, will I am sure give you a good testimonial. She uses it, and recommends it to her pupils. Yours truly, MRS. C. M. BORDNER.

Schuylkill Haven, Pa., Aug. 24, 1897.

Mr. Hall:

Dear Sir: Will you allow me the privilege of congratulating you upon the merits of your Roman Gold? I have been using same for three years, and can truthfully and religiously say it is a far superior quality and works to a much better advantage than any gold I have ever used. It has always proved perfectly satisfactory in every particular; never fails, "economy is wealth," and I feel it a duty and take special pleasure to recommend it to all who are interested in china painting. I can assure you no other but Hall's Roman Gold can ever grace my studio. Very sincerely yours,

ELIZABETH SHANNON ZULICH

Montpelier, Vt., June 12, 1897.

Mr. Hall:

Dear Sir: Enclosed please find draft for $7.20 for which please send by return mail one dozen boxes of your Superior Roman Gold. My pupils wished to try the .... gold, which they sell at 50 cents per box, so I have had my last gold from there, but we find that it is not so cheap as yours after all. I return to you feeling better satisfied than before. Yours sincerely, MRS. A. O. CUMMINS.

144 Pine St., Portland, Me., Aug. 24, 1897.
Mr. J. F. Hall:
Dear Sir: I have never used a gold which gave me so much satisfaction as yours. I have tried a great many makes, and always gladly came back to yours. In color it is unsurpassed, and it always spends well. I will always be ready to recommend Hall's Roman Gold as long as it keeps to its present quality. Respectfully, MRS. MARGARET S. DAVIS.

Allentown, Pa., Aug. 28, 1897.
Mr. James F. Hall:
Dear Sir: I have used your Prepared Roman Gold and Bronzes for sixteen years. Both my pupils and myself can highly recommend it, both for quality, quantity and durability. Very respectfully, MISS EMMA J. KNAUSS.

Whiteman, Mass., Aug. 28, 1897.
Mr. James F. Hall:
Dear Sir: I have used your Gold for about two years with perfect satisfaction. I have used many kinds of gold, but yours gives better results than any I have had experience with. Respectfully yours, ETHEL S. NASH.

Newburyport, Mass., Aug. 28, 1897.
Mr. James F. Hall:
Dear Sir: I have used your Roman Gold for several years, and like it very much. I have not used many other kinds, as yours has always been so satisfactory. Yours respectfully, MISS MARTHA F. JAQUES.

Studio, No. 58 E. 96th St., New York, 1897.
Mr. J. F. Hall:
Dear Sir: Both myself and pupils are highly pleased with your Gold. We have found it at all times very satisfactory. It is always used in my studio, and my pupils as well as myself would not use any other. You can readily perceive how well satisfied I am with your Gold by the large quantity which I use each year. Respectfully yours, ELLA HEYMAN.

York, Pa., Aug. 24, 1897.
Mr. Hall:
Dear Sir: In regard to your Roman Gold must say I'm so well pleased with it that I have no desire to use any other, as long as it gives such satisfactory results, and the pupils are all praising it. You are at perfect liberty to use my name. Very respectfully, ANNIE O. HANTZ.

Studio 96, 5th Ave., New York.
Mr. James F. Hall:
Dear Sir: Your Roman Gold and your other combinations of gold, silver and liquid lustres have been in every way satisfactory to me. They fire

well with very light heat, and yet they stand a strong fire. My pupils like
the Gold and praise it for quality, quantity and color. We show our sin-
cere appreciation of its uniform excellence by continuing to use it. Sincerely yours, MRS. FANNY ROWELL PRIESTMAN.
Superintendent Hasbrouck School of Art, President Jersey City Keramic
Art Club, Corresponding Secretary National League of Mineral Painters,
Art Editor of the Ceramic Monthly.

Studio, 317 Spring St., Portland, Me. Mr. James F. Hall:
Dear Sir: I find both your Roman and Hard Gold entirely satisfactory.
I have used them for several years, and the result is always the same. Sin-
cerely, GERTRUDE MILLET.

Lynn, Mass., Aug. 23, 1897.
Mr. James F. Hall:
Dear Sir: I don't remember how long I have been using your Gold. I
have not even tried any other kind since; have always used it with satisfactory results. I think it superior to any other gold I ever used as to
quality and quantity, and can highly recommend it to anyone, which I have
done several times. My orders have always been promptly attended to and
cannot report an instance where I have been inconvenienced. Wishing you
continued success, respectfully, MRS. S. E. BLANCHARD.

Boston, Mass., Aug., 1897.
Mr. J. F. Hall:
Dear Sir: I have found your Gold very satisfactory. I would certainly
ask for nothing better. You have always filled my orders very promptly. If
you wish you can use my name in your testimonials. Very truly,
ELIZABETH P. CARTER.

Bellefontaine, O., Aug. 30, 1897.
Mr. James F. Hall:
Dear Sir: I am very glad to tell you that I am very much pleased
with your Roman Gold, and I have found it much more satisfactory in
every way than any other "gold" I have used. I am perfectly willing you should
use my name in reference to your Gold. Yours truly,
MRS. CARRIE BUTLER.

Rome, N. Y., Aug. 25, 1897.
Mr. James F. Hall:
Dear Sir: I have used your Roman Gold for the past two years with
perfect success. I find it satisfactory in every respect, and can heartily
recommend it. I have tried nearly every gold in the market, and prefer
yours to all others. Yours respectfully, MISS A. D. MITCHELL.

Beech Cliff, Pa., Aug. 28, 1897.

Mr. J. F. Hall:

Dear Sir: I consider your Roman Gold more satisfactory in every respect than any other gold that I have used. It goes farther, and has a finer appearance when burnished. I never use any other gold if I can get "Hall's" and would recommend it to all teachers and decorators.. Yours truly,

ANNA ROSBOROUGH.

Wilkesbarre, Pa., Aug. 29, 1897.

Mr. James F. Hall:

Dear Sir: I use your Roman Gold exclusively, finding it satisfactory in every respect and take pleasure in recommending it. Very sincerely,

ESTHER KLINE.

Wilkesbarre, Pa., Sept. 1, 1897.

Mr. Hall: It gives me great pleasure to recommend your Gold. I think it superior in color, quality and quantity to any gold manufactured. I have used it for years with perfect success. Yours truly,

GERTRUDE HAND.

New Hartford, Conn., Aug. 24, 1897.

Mr. James F. Hall:

Dear Sir: I have bought your Gold, and no other for the past four years and it is needless to say that I consider it superior to any other. I usually buy it in the jars, which I think is very convenient, besides keeping the gold in a moist condition. You are perfectly welcome to refer anyone to me regarding the Gold. Yours respectfully,   MRS. CLARA G. CHAPMAN.

Blairstown, N. J., Aug., 1897.

Mr. Hall:

Dear Sir: Your Roman Gold has given me entire satisfaction in every way. I can recommend it as the best I have ever used.

HUDDIE ANDRESS.

Dover, N. H., Aug. 29, 1897.

Mr. Hall:

Dear Sir: Mrs. Bacon and her pupils are highly pleased with the results they get from your "Roman Gold." In fact, no one could induce them to even try any other make, and so long as yours gives the same perfect satisfaction she will purchase no other. Respectfully yours, BACON, THE JEWELER.

Staunton, Va., Aug., 1897.

Mr. J. F. Hall:

Dear Sir: I am perfectly willing that you should use this testimonial in regard to your Gold. I have always found it most satisfactory in   every way, and it is far the best I have ever used (and I have tried many different kinds), but so long as I can get your Gold no other will ever grace my studio.

Yours sincerely,

MRS. J. B. CATLETT.

Westbrook, Me., Aug. 25, 1897.

Mr. James F. Hall:

Dear Sir: Have used your Gold for two years or more. Like it better than any other I have tried. Am willing that you should use my indorsement to that effect. Please send by return mail one dozen boxes, eight Roman and four Hard, and oblige yours respectfully,

MRS. M. A. WORTHLEY.

Bramwell, W. Va., Aug. 26, 1897.

Mr. Hall:

Dear Sir: I take pleasure in sending you my testimonial in favor of your Roman Gold. Having used it successfully for a number of years can most truthfully acknowledge its merits. It has always given entire satisfaction to myself and all who have used it with me, and it cannot receive too much praise. Your truly,   MRS. H. P. WITHINGTON.

Bramwell, W. Va.

Mr. Hall:

Dear Sir: It gives me great pleasure to testify to the perfect satisfaction I have found in the use of "Hall's Roman Gold." I could not find a gold whose lustre and richness surpass it, and the quantity in each box is more than I have been able to get elsewhere. After an experience of over ten years with the different "golds" in the market I think I shall always try to get "Hall's Gold."   MRS. R. H. PATTERSON.

Fort Smith, Ark., Aug., 1897.

Mr. Hall:

Dear Sir: I consider your Gold has no superior, and in proof of my opinion will say I have never used any other since trying your Gold.

MRS. WM. A. FALCONER.

Minneapolis, Minn., Aug., 23, 1897.

Mr. James F. Hall:

Dear Sir: I am more than pleased with "The Hall's Roman Gold," after using it a year or more, and take pleasure in recommending it to any who may contemplate purchasing. Yours respectfully,

ELIZABETH BOFFERDING.

Sunbury, Pa., Aug. 30, 1897.

Mr. James F. Hall:

Dear Sir: For nearly five years I have used your Gold and Bronze, and find them equal in quality and superior in quantity to any among the large number I have tried, and I gladly recommend it. Very truly yours,

MILDRED O. COBURN.

George's Mills, N. H., Aug. 29, 1897.
Mr. James F. Hall:
Dear Sir: It gives me great pleasure to state that I have used your Gold for several years, and consider it superior to any other. In fact, it is so perfectly satisfactory in every respect that I never use any other except when yours is unobtainable. Very truly yours

MRS. WALTER F. AYERS.

Bridgeport, Conn., Aug. 31, 1897.
Having used for several years for myself and pupils the Roman Gold made by James F. Hall it gives me pleasure to speak of its perfect success. It is unanimously thought in my studio to be far the best and richest in lustre of any gold upon the market. Respectfully yours,

CARRIE B. DOREMUS.

Norristown, Pa., Aug. 31, 1897.
Mr. Hall.
Dear Sir: Will be very glad to recommend your Roman Gold. Have used it for a number of years with perfect satisfaction in every respect. Have tried other makes of gold, but do not consider that they can be compared with your Gold. Yours truly,   M. BLANCHE LENZI.

Saginaw, Mich., Aug. 27, 1897.
Mr. James F. Hall:
Dear Sir: I am very glad to give a testimonial with regard to your Roman Gold. I have used it exclusively for several years, finding it entirely satisfactory. Very truly yours,   WINIFRED SMITH.

New Haven, Conn., Aug. 30, 1897.
Mr. James F. Hall:
Dear Sir: Have just returned from my vacation and found the Gold in readiness. I thank you for your promptness. Was afraid I might be obliged to purchase other gold before yours came. I am better pleased with your Roman Gold than any other, and most all of my pupils also use it. I say a good word for your Gold everywhere I go, for the results have always been satisfactory. I am perfectly willing that you should use my name. Very truly yours,   JENNIE E. HANSON.

Haverhill, Mass., Sept. 2, 1897.
Mr. James F. Hall:
Dear Sir: Both myself and pupils use Hall's Roman Gold entirely and

find it gives better satisfaction than any we have ever used. Yours sincerely,
MRS. H. C. SNELLING.

Dallas, Texas.

Mr. Hall: I take great pleasure in saying that to me your Roman Gold has been of all others the most satisfactory. I think it will lay more surface than any other, and fires with more uniformity than any other I have tried. I gave a box the other day to a decorator to try, and she was immensely pleased with it, and will use it altogether hereafter.
ELIZABETH P. KIEST.

Galion, O., Aug. 29, 1897.
Mr. James F. Hall:
Dear Sir: I find your Gold quite satisfactory in every respect. Have used it exclusively for the past three years, both in my own work and that of my pupils. Respectfully,
ANNA L. STIEFEL.

Pontiac, Ill., Aug., 1897.
Mr. James F. Hall:
Dear Sir: I find your Roman Gold more satisfactory in every respect than any other gold I have used. I have used your Gold for nearly seven years, and in that time have tried eight different makes, but have not found any I like as well as the Gold prepared by you. I prefer it because it is ground so very smooth and fine that it can be applied to large surfaces and burnish perfectly smooth; also your Gold has never varied in quality or quantity. I could not wish for anyone to be more honest or prompt in filling their orders. My pupils are always enthusiastic over your Gold and never want to try any other. You may refer to me, also publish my testimonial. The above will also apply to your White Enamel. It is certainly as good as your Gold.
THE MISSES WOODROW,
Per Ida Woodrow.

Topeka, Kan., Aug. 26, 1897.
Mr. James F. Hall:
Dear Sir: I am perfectly willing that you should refer to me in regard to your Roman Gold, for I have always found it to be perfectly satisfactory in every respect. Have used it since 1890, and have found it superior to all others, both in quality and quantity. Your Gold when burnished presents a rich, metallic, brilliant surface very suggestive of the solid ore. Wishing you success, respectfully,
MRS. E. M. KALE.

Lynn, Mass., Aug. 24, 1897.
Mr. Hall:
Dear Sir: I am pleased to say that I like your Roman and Hard Gold better than any I ever tried. The same I can say of my class, who use it

wholly. I have used it now for a long time, and wish for nothing better. I used to send by order with Mrs. Crane's, but since she has given up painting on account of sickness have been sending with Mrs. Blanchard.   Sincerely yours,   MRS. J. G. BUZZELL.

Allentown, Pa., Sept., 1897.
Mr. J. F. Hall:
    Dear Sir: I am very glad indeed to be able to testify to the superiority of Hall's Roman Gold over any other that I have ever used, and I have tried several others, and having used several hundred dollars' worth of Hall's I certainly ought to be able to   test   its   worth.   Indeed,   I   consider   your   second   grade   of   Gold   equal   if   not   superior   to   any other   first   grade   I   have   ever   used.   The gold on my own work   has often been commented upon, and I have been asked repeatedly for your address by other china painters, that they might send for same.   You are at liberty to use my name as you wish in your catalogue, for I would like it known to all who take an interest in china painting that I consider Hall's Golds superior to any in the market.   Most respectfully,
                                    HARRIET A. HILL,
    Ceramic Art Teacher, Female College, Allentown, Pa.

                    ¡   Homer, La., Sept., 1897.
Mr. J. F. Hall:
    Dear Sir: With pleasure I state that I have used your Roman Gold in my class for years, and both myself and pupils have always found it most satisfactory in every respect. Very truly yours,   E. A. TRAYLOR.

                    Whatcom, Washington, Aug. 30, 1897.
Mr. J. F. Hall:
    Dear Sir: I take pleasure in recommending your Roman Gold. I have used it in my studio for a number of years, and prefer it to any gold in the market. It has the advantage over other golds in being easily applied, which is a great advantage to beginners and amateurs. Yours respectfully,
                                    JESSIE C. TEMPLIN,
                                    Studio B. B. Building.

Hall's Roman Gold and Bronzes are for sale, at retail, by the following Agents.

PENNSYLVANIA.

F, Weber & Co , 1125 Chestnut street., Philad'a.
Ripka & Co., 132 South Eleventh street, Philad'a.
A. E. O'Hara, 1222 Columbia avenue, Philad'a.
Gano & Costen, 53 E. Main street. Norristown.
A. Kline, 26 S. Main street, Wilkes-Barre.
O. T. Chambers, Druggist, Honesdale.
S. L. Hagenbaugh, 10 N. Franklin street, Wilkes-Barre.
A, B. Purple, Columbia.
W. S. Rishton, Main street, Bloosmburg.
A. D. Thomas & Co., 130 W. Main street, Plymonth.
Turner & Kantner, 12th street, Altoona
Chas. L. Griffin, 209 Wyoming avenue, Scranton.
M. Norton, 322 Lackawanna avenue, Scranton,
Chas. Wallace Quicksell, 11 S. Main street, Wilkes-Barre.
J. Alfred Shafer, 33 N. 7th street, Allentown.
Turner & Gordon, Druggists, Towanda.
N, R, Wendelboe, 209 Liberty street, Warren.

NEW YORK CITY.

Favor, Ruhl & Co., 140 Sullivan street.
Devoe & Raynolds Co.,Corner Fulton and William street.
Mrs. Fanny R. Priestman, 96 Fifth avenue.
Miss Ella Heyman, 58 E. 96th street.

NEW YORK.

Rowney & Horton, 56 Genesee street, Utica.
E. F. Bloomer, Binghampton.

MAINE.

C. H. Blackington, 217 Water street, Augusta.
Miss G. C. Millet, 317 Spring street, Portland.

INDIANA.

J. M. Shank, China Dealer, Union City.
Mrs. J. Skillman, Union City.

CONNECTICUT.

Mr. Ed. W. Merriman, 39 N. Main street, Bristol.
Mrs. C· B. Doremus, 77 West avenue, Bridgeport.
Miss Jennie E. Hauson, Studio 58 Prince street, New Haven.
The Bonner Preston Company, 329 Main street, Hartford.
J. H. Eckhardt & Co., 231 Main street, Hartford,

ILLINOIS·

A. H. Abbott & Co., Chicago,
Mrs. Jennie B. Williams, 245 Oakland Boulevard,Chicago.
Mrs Ida Woodrow, Pontiac.

MARYLAND.

Hirshberg, Hollander & Co., Lexington street, Baltimore.
F. Weber & Co., Baltimore.

KANSAS.

Mr. J. C. Armstrong, 206 Main street, Ottawa.
Mrs. E. M. Kate, 619 Taylor street, Topeka.
W. W. Morris, 23 Opera Block, Eureka.
Mr. T. C. Hughes, Druggist, Osawatomie.

OHIO.

Col's Paint Manufacturing Company, 15 W. Broad street, Columbus.
Mr. Ralph S. Tebbutt, 636 Market street, Sandusky.
Mr. H. Tischendorf, 1146 Oak street, Columbus.
Miss Carrie Butler, 500 Sandusky avenue, Bellefontaine.
Miss Anna L. Stiefel, Galion.
McBroom & Co., 391 Bond street, Cleveland.

MASSACHUSETTS.

Frost & Adams, 37 Cornhill, Boston.
Mrs. Martha Green, 11 Vinal avenue, Somerville.
Mrs. S. C. Blanchard, 33 Atlantic street, Lynn.
Mrs. E. P. Carter, 68 W. Rutland Square, Boston.
Mrs. H. O. Crane, 26 W. Baltimore street, Lynn.
Miss Gertrude Cheney Davis, Studio 64, 374 Boylston street, Boston.
Miss Ruth Farnsworth, 119 W. Springfield street, Boston.
Mrs. Mary P. Gardner, 263 Washington street, Haverhill.
Miss Martha F. Jacques, 9 Purchase street, Newburyport.
Mrs. Charlotte C. Lummus, 229 Ocean street, Lynn.
Mrs. A· M. Noah, 46 Beverly street, Boston.
Miss Ethel S. Nash, Whitman.

Mrs H. S. Snelling, Haverhill.
Mrs. A. F. Williams, 52 Roger avenue, Lynn.

NORTH CAROLINA.
Mr. R. A. Ross, Bookseller and Stationer, Charlotte.

VERMONT.
E. E. Clarkson & Co., Burlington.
Geo. T. Collins. 17 Merchants' Row, Rutland.
Van Doorin & Morris, 76 Main street, Brattleboro.

GEORGIA.
McEvoy, Sanders & Co., 572 Cherry street, Macon·
Holt's Art and Stationery Company, 365 Second street, Macon.

COLORADO.
Mr. N. F. Gross. 2048 Lincoln avenue, Denver.

VIRGINIA.
The Craig Art Company, 115 E. Broad street Richmond.
Henson & Co., Bedford City.
Dr. N. Wayt & Brother, Staunton.

NEW HAMPSHIRE.
Mr. C. E. Bacon, Jeweler, Dover.

MICHIGAN.
Thomas Cooke & Co., 106-108 Huron avenue, Port Huron.
J. W. Goulding & Co., 206-208 Huron avenue, Port Huron.
John Schmelzer, 511-513 Genesee avenue, Saginaw.

TEXAS.
Mr. C. M. League, 2015 Market street, Galveston.
Mrs. W. F. Ayers, 1512 Avenue H, Galveston.
Mrs. E. P. Kiest, 219 Crutcher street, Dallas.
Peyton & Co., Belton.

ARKANSAS.
Decorative Art Rooms, Little Rock.

MISSOURI.
Mr. George F. Mitchell, New Ridge Building, Kansas City.
Miss Berinice Johnson, Carrolton,
Mrs. Anna Waller, 400 W.16th street, Sedalia.
A. W. Perry & Son, 206 Broadway, Sedalia.

ENAMEL POWDER COLORS.

FOR PAINTING ON CHINA FINELY GROUND AND FLUXED.

	Per Bottle.		Per Bottle.
Ruby	25	Night Green	10
Maroon	25	Gordon Green (medium)	10
Purple	20	No. 1 Green	10
Best English Rose	10	No. 2 green (grass)	10
Lilac	10	Apple Green (light)	10
Violet	10	Emerald Green	10
Filet Red (French)	10	Olive Green	10
Light Red	10	Sap Green	10
Pompadour	10	Brown Green	10
Indigo Blue(deep)	10	Yellow (for mixing)	10
No. 1 Blue (rich)	10	Silver Yellow	10
Turkish Blue	10	Albert Yellow	10
Turquoise Blue	10	Egg Yellow	10
Dark Brown	10	Amber	10
Light Brown	10	Gold Bud Yellow	10
Hair Brown	10	Orange	10
Auburn Brown	10	Purple Brown	10
Russet Brown	10	Violet of Iron	10
Lustre Brown	10	No. 3 Turquoise	10
No. 1 Brown (red)	10	Unique	10
Florentine Green (dark)	10	Black (brilliant)	10
No. 12 Green (dark)	10	Flux	10
Yellow Ochre	10	Best White Enamel	10
Peach Blossom	10	Delft Blue	10
Capucine Red	10	Coalport Green (medium	
Deep Red Brown	10	shade)	10
Dover Green	10	Light Carmine	10
		Ivory	10

HOW TO PAINT ON CHINA,

Several eloquent, and also some "dry-as-dust" books, have been written on the theory of painting on china. We are, however, acquainted with very few books containing precisely those explanations of the processes and materials employed in this beautiful art, which we believe can be given and would greatly assist, not only the student but the general public to understand and appreciate the work more than it is. To supply (from practical-acquaintance with painting on china) such information is my chief aim. It is not my intention, however, to write a book on "How to Paint on China," but to simply give a brief practical lesson. I shall endeavor to put the matter in as plain and simple a form as I possibly can. It is my intention principally to teach the pupil the method of mixing and painting with powder colors, but at the same time I do not wish to hold them to powder colors entirely. I leave it to their own discretion whether they prefer the tubes or powders. Here is a scale of powder colors, with the corresponding color in tubes A. LaCroix. Ruby (Ruby Purple); Rose Color (Carmine); Orange (Orange Yellow); Yellow (Yellow for mixing); No. 1 Blue (Deep Ultramarine) Turkish Blue (Light Blue); Filet Red (Capucine Red); Light Brown (Brown 108); Black (Ivory Black); Dark Brown (Dark Brown) No. 12 Green (Chrome Green); Apple Green (Apple Green); Brown Green (Brown Green); White Enamel (Permanent White). It is a great mistake to suppose that powder and tube colors cannot be mixed together. better results are very often attained by mixing one with the other, and it sometimes is necessary to add a little powder to the tube colors, for you will often find on taking the color from the tube that it is too oily. Whenever this happens add a little of the same color in powder, for instance, yellow to mixing yellow: Rose color to Carmine; No. 12 Green to Chrome Green, etc. Add a drop of turpentine (no oil) and mix well together with a steel palette knife. While the color is spread out somewhat on the palette, breathe slightly into it and mix again, then place the color in as small a space as possible and put at the head of the palette. If the color is left spread out it will soon dry and get fat and sticky, and will not be in fit condition for working. All the colors must be treated the same way—a drop of turpentine added, mixed, and breathed into, then mixed again and placed next to the other color in order, until you have all the colors mixed that you require. If the tube colors are not too oily the powder need not be added.

Powder colors are rapidly taking the place of the ready mixed colors in tubes, and I strongly advise all beginners to start in with the former, for tube colors although ready mixed, are not, as most people believe, ready for use; they require softening with a little turpentine or lavender oil, and mixing thoroughly with the palette knife. This takes up quite as much time as the powder color would to mix. All the latter requires extra is a drop or so of thick or fat oil; they require no grinding, simply mix well together as you would the tube colors.

The way the colors are mixed and the condition they are kept in depends almost entirely on the success of the work, so I will now give an easy and practical system of mixing.

We will suppose that we have before us all necessary articles, for instance: Powder colors, thick oil, lavender oil, turpentine, a 6x6-inch glass slab and a steel palette knife. Now take a little powder color and thick oil, two parts of color to one of oil, mix well together, then dip the end of the knife in turpentine and mix again. While the color is spread out somewhat breathe slightly into it and mix again, but as little as possible after breathing into it; scrape the color together and put in as small a space as possible at the head of the slab. Breathing into the color prevents it from flowing and at the same time keeps it in condition. If this is not done it will dry very quickly and get sticky. Lavender oil may be used in place of turpentine if you wish the colors to keep moist longe Mix all the colors that you require before attempting to paint, and place them in regular order at the head of the slab, each one in as small a space as possible.

Mixed Tints. It is always advisable to mix the pure tints first, as the mixed shades may then more readily be produced. Quite a variety of tints may be obtained from six to eight of the pure colors by mixing one with another; the most beautiful grays are only to be got by mixing; it is quite useless to buy those ready mixed. Take equal parts of Turkish blue and orange, add a touch of rose color and mix well together. If a bluer gray is required add more blue. No. 1 blue and orange, or light brown, gives a deeper gray; blue and yellow will also produce a gray, but of a greenish shade. Ruby and rose color may also be mixed with very good results. while ruby and blue make a beautiful purple, and with more blue added produces violet or lilac. Add orange to light-brown to lighten it, and yellow to range. All the shades of green that are required for china painting can be got from two pure colors and yellow. No. 12 green is dark, and apple green light. By mixing the two together in different proportions produce of course different shades, and by adding yellow to apple green the lightest possible shades may be had. Greens of different shades are also mixed with orange or light brown. Green and blue are also very useful colors for use in foliage. Orange mixed with a little rose color is very useful for new shoots, especially in the foliage of roses. Black is the body of all colors, but must be used with great judgment; it may be used with most every color in producing grays.

No regular formula need be followed in regard to mixing of neutral tints for a touch of ruby, rose, purple or lilac when added to a green will give most all the neutrals that are needed in foliage.

No. 12 green and light brown makes brown green for shading leaves.

There are, it must be understood, some colors that when mixed together for one fire will not have the same effect as when one is painted over the other at two firings. For example: rose color and orange when mixed for one fire will not be as pure and clean as when one color is painted over the other at two fires. The same with grays over other colors—they are not as transparent.

All plainting on china should have at least two firings. In the first painting the colors must not be put on too thick, especially on French china. If so, the chances are that in the second firing they will scale, and whenever this happens it is impossible to repair the damage, for the oftener the china is fired the more the colors will scale. Of course very good results are often got with one fire, but the work is generally executed by persons that understand the manipulation of the colors for one firing. If you intend a painting to only have one fire, paint for one fire—that is, finish in detail all you wish to. If the painting is delicate all through, and after firing you think it could be improved by a few touches, there is really no risk in having it re-fired, but if the colors are thick in places, especially in the pinks, violets or lilacs, do not risk another fire, for it is far better to sacrifice a little detail than to ruin the whole painting. I refer to French or German china. English china may be fired as often as you see fit without risk of the colors scaling. China with the least imperfections should always be selected for painting in enamel colors, for as they are transparent all defects in the china will show through the colors after firing.

Before we begin to paint, a good idea would be to suggest some simple design—take for instance a wild rose with two or three open flowers, a few buds, very little foliage and a graceful spray of forget-me-nots running through. This I believe will be a very good subject for the beginner.

We will now suppose that we have the design ready sketched (or traced) in India ink or pencil (if India ink is used apply the lines as delicate as possible), and that we have before us all necessary articles, colors, oils, brushes, etc. Commence with the open flowers using a No. 2 or 3 square shader, dip the brush in turpentine, then wipe on a soft rag, merely leaving sufficient turpentine in the brush to keep the hairs in close contact with each other; now dip the point of the brush in thick oil, taking up very little, work the point of the brush in the rose color (simply at the edge of it) until the oil is mixed sufficiently with color, now paint in the open flowers, applying the color in thin washes, leaving the china for the high lights; a little more color may now be taken up with the brush for the buds. The thicker the color is applied the less oil must be used. Next to follow in order are the forget-me-nots; take a No. 1 square shader and treat it the same as the brush used for the rose, but with less soil. Use Turkish blue applied a little thicker than the rose color (each petal must be formed with one stroke of the brush), put in a thin wash of yellow to the centre of the roses and forget-me-nots, always using plenty of oil when the colors are to be in thin washes. It must be understood, however, that the brush must never be kept too full of color so that it reaches to the quill—the idea is to keep the color at the point of the brush, and to dip in the color repeatedly; now with the No. 3 brush paint in the largest leaves in the foliage, using No. 12 green, and apple green pure for the more decided shades. For the small leaves use a No. 1 or 2 brush, put in a few of the most delicate and small leaves with yellow and orange, apple green, orange and rose color; light greens made neutral with a touch of rose color, blue, or ruby. Use a medium tracer for the stems which may be painted with apple green and yellow mixed. A spot of light green must now be added to the centre of the roses, and the stamens painted with orange, or orange and a little light brown.

We will now treat the design for the second painting. If it is to be finished for one firing allow the first painting to dry thoroughly, but if it is intended to have two firings it may be fired at once. Remix the pure colors on the slab, add a drop or two of turpentine and breathe into as before. Use turpentine or lavender with the colors in the second painting. With a No. 2 brush put a few sharp touches and broad shades in the roses with pure rose color, a shade of gray (blue and orange), here and there to give depth. Shade the spot of green in the centre with brown green (No. 12 green and light brown). Shade the stamens with light brown and put in a few very fine lines with the tracer from the spot in the centre to the stamens. A shade of gray over one side of the yellow gives depth. Shade the forget-me-nots with Turkish blue and put in the centres a spot of light brown. Finish in detail as much as possible the largest leaves with a No. 2 or 3 brush, using brown green, different strengths. A little apple green added to the brown green may be used to vary the shading somewhat, also to shade the smaller leaves. Use a tracer for the sharp touches at the edges, also to finish the stems. The foliage painted in neutral tints must be shaded with the same. Use light brown, and light brown and rose color to shade the stems.

A few touches of white enamel may now be applied, but it must be used very sparingly, as too much gives coarseness to the work. Mix with a very little thick oil and turpentine and breathe into it like the colors, apply it with a tracer in spots or drag it from the brush. Great care must be taken in mixing the enamel, see that the palette and knife are perfectly clean and free from any color whatever, or the enamel will not fire clean and white. Wash all color brushes out thoroughly in turpentine, and wipe them on a soft rag, do not use soap and water, as that will soon ruin them.

Enamel powder colors may be painted over a background of either matt white, satin finish, or vellum, and is very effective, the background must of course be fired first.

I trust this little practical information will be of some benefit to the beginner, and that she will not become discouraged if her first work should not turn out just as she anticipated, for we are well aware that to become an adept in any class of art requires a great deal of practice.

JAMES F. HALL.

HALL'S

New Ceramic Colors.

PUT UP IN GLASS JARS:

Mixed with an entirely New Preparation of Fat Oil ready for immediate use.

These colors will not harden while in the jar.   A tint or background painted with these colors, will remain soft and moist for any desired length of time, and therefore will permit the blending of one with the other.

Full practical instruction for the mixing of different tints, etc. will be sent with first order.   The following set of Ceramic Colors, Oil and Brushes, will be found to answer all ordinary needs, and upon receipt of $4.00 will be sent, with practical instructions, post-paid to any part of the United States or Canada.

Per Jar.		Per Jar.	
Ruby	50	Light Brown 20	
Best Ross	25	Filet Red 20	
No. 1 Blue, dark	24	Mixing Yellow 20	
Turkish Blue, light	25	Albert Yellow 25	
Florentine Green, dark . . .	20	Orange 20	
Apple Green, light	20	Brown Green 20	
Dark Brown	20	Black . . . : 20	

Fat Oil specially prepared, to use with Ceramic Colors, ½ ounce,   15

SPECIAL FIRST QUALITY BRUSHES.

For Painting with Hall's Ceramic Colors.

	No. 1	No. 2	No. 3	No. 4
Flat Shaders, each	08	10	10	10
Tracers or Liners, each	10	8	7	

Sample Plate, showing the above 14 colors fired in . . . . . 50 cents
Or sent by Mail, postage paid. 60 cents.

ENAMEL TINTING COLORS.

FINELY GROUND IN OIL, READY FOR USE, IN ½ OUNCE BOTTLES.

Price, 15 cents.   By Mail, 17 cents.

Bright Vellum.	Crimson.
Buff	Turquoise Blue.
Salmbn.	Purple Brown.
Rose Pink·	Egg Yellow.
Apple Green	Olive Green.
Turkish Blue·	No. 1 Green.
Violet of Iron.	No. 2 Green.
Turquoise.	Emerald Green
Grey.	Sap Green
Celadon.	Gordon Green.
No. 1 Fawn.	Turquoise Green
Lustre Brown.	Chrome Green.
Violet	Amber.
Light Celadon.	Lilac.
Ivory	Lavender.
Coalport Green.	Peach Blossom
Old Rose.	Dover Green.

See Diections for Tinting with Matt or Gouche Colors

OPAQUE ENAMELS FOR RELIEF WORK,

FINELY GROUND.

Price, 10 cents per Bottle.

Turquoise.	Coral Red.
Pink, (Rose.)	White.

Tourquoise and Coral Red will stand on Roman Gold and Bronzes after the golds have been fired. Mix the enamels with Hall's Relief Medium and turpentine and apply in relief; do not fire them a second time when they are applied to French or German china.

Enamel Powder Colors for Groundlaying.

FINELY GROUND AND * LAWNED.

	Per Packet		Per Packet
Ruby	25	No. 1 Green	10
Maroon	25	No. 2 Green	10
No. 5 Pink	10	Gordon Green	10
No. 26 Pink	10	Turquoise Green	10
French White (light Pink)	10	Olive Green	10
No. 1 Fawn	10	Apple Green	10
Chinese Yellow	10	Celadon	10
Vermillion	10	Celeste	10
Emerald Green	10	Light Celeste	10
Lilac	10	Light Celadon	10
Salmon	10	No. 2 Turquoise	10
Filet Red	10	Lustre Brown	10
Light Red	10	Russett Brown	10
Buff	10	French Grey	10
Indigo Blue	10	Amber	10
Turkish Blue	10	Chocolate	10
Turquoise Blue	10	Lavender	10
Blue Green	15	Canary	10
Auburn Brown	10	Golden Fawn	10
Matt Vellum	10	Coalport Green	10

* Having been passed through a silk lawn.
  For directions, see next page.

How to Groundlay with Enamel Powder Colors

Take equal parts of groundlaying oil and spirits of turpentine, mix well together in a clean saucer with a steel palette knife, and with a medium sized tinting brush apply a thin, even coat of the oil to the piece of china you desire to groundlay, the brush must be worked well into the oil, and enough taken up to cover the article, the china must be perfectly clean, free from dust or lint, before you apply the oil. Lay aside the article for five minutes, when it will become tacky, and in the meantime procure a ball of cotton the size of a tea cup, and a piece of soft linen twelve inches long and six inches wide, double this to form a square and tie in the cotton to form a ball of six inches in circumference, if any larger, (the pad as it is called), will be too soft, and if smaller, too hard. With this, pad the oil on the article all over until the oil is perfectly even ; to test this, allow the light to shine on the surface and if there are no marks in the oil it is all right.

Care must be taken to strike the oil with the pad perfectly straight, for by allowing it to slide in any way on the oil it leaves marks, that when it is fired gives the ground a cloudy appearance.

The strength of color required depends entirely on the thickness of the oil and the time it is allowed to stand before applying the color.

The proportion of oil and turpentine that I gave, and by allowing it to stand five minutes after padding, will give a medium strength of color. If a very light shade is wanted add two of turpentine to one of oil, and allow the article after padding to stand from ten to twenty minutes. If a dark or thick color is required, use two of oil to one of turpentine, and after it is padded apply the color at once.

To apply the color.—Take a package of color and empty the contents on a large plate or dish, and with a piece of fine cotton, (jewelers is the best), take up as much color as possible and let it fall lightly on the oil, follow the color with the cotton, always keeping some color between the cotton and oil; if you allow the cotton to come in contact with the oil it will mark it and spoil the ground. Hold the article in the left hand over the plate or dish to save the color from spilling. After the oil is well covered with color a little more pressure with the cotton may be applied, so as to get the ground uniform. The ground must have a dull or matt appearance; if any oily marks appear, apply the color again, dust off all remaining color that has not adhered to the oil with a clean piece of cotton.

To Erase the Color.—Sketch the design over the ground with pale India ink, then go over the outlines with a sharp pointed stick, and remove the inner color of the design with a blunt, soft stick, dust all bits of color off with a piece of cotton, or a camel hair brush.

By allowing the ground to dry thoroughly, the first painting may be done before it is fired.

LACROIX ENAMEL COLORS.

FOR PAINTING ON GLAZED CHINA, EARTHENWARE, ETC.

In Tubes, like Moist Colors, Ready for Use.

FOR PAINTING.

Blacks

Per Tube.		Per Tube.
Ivory Black 16	Raven Black 20
Brunswick Black 43	Outlining Black 23

Blues

Blue, No. 29, for Earthenware,16	Light Sky Blue 20
Dark Blue 16	Sky Blue 20
Deep Blue 20	Victoria Blue, or Ordinaire . 16
Deep Ultramarine 28	Old Llue 15
Two Fire Blue 20	Delft Blue 16
Common Blue 16	Cornflower Blue 20
Old Rouen Blue 16	Air Blue 23
Sevres Blue 28	Old Holland Blue. 20

Browns

Brown, No. 3 20	Sepia 20
Brown, No. 4 or 17 20	Yellow Brown 20
Brown, M. or 108 20	Black Brown 20
Dark Brown 20	Chestnut Brown 20
Deep Red Brown 20	Otto Brown 20
Light Brown 20	Van Dyke Brown 20
Gillyflower Brown 20	

Greens

Apple Green 16	Deep Green 20
Brown Green, No. 6 20	Emerald Stone Green . . . 20
Chrome Green, Mo. 3 B . .2o	Grass Green, No 5 20
Bronze Green 28	Green, No. 36 T 20
Dark Green, No. 7 20	Sap Green 20
Deep Blue Green 28	Duck Green 20
Deep Chrome Green . . .20	Moss Green, V 20
Moss Green J. (yellowish) . 20	Olive Green 25
Night Green 28	Shading Green 28
Coalport Green, light 23	Blue Green, light 35
" " dark 23	Blue Green, dark 35
Rose Leaf Green 23	

Grays

Gray, No. 1, light	20	Pearl Gaay, No. 9	20
Gray, No. 2	20	Warm Gaay	20
Neutral Gray	20	Gray for Flowers	23
Gray for Flesh	23	Gold Gray	35
Royal Copenhagen Gray	28		

Royal Copenhagen Gray, warm . . 28

Reds

Capucine Red	20	Orange Red	23
Bengal Rose	20	Bright Red	23
Flame Red	23	Japan Rose	28
Laky Red	23	Chinese Rose	20

Pompadour Red, No. 23 23

Carmines

Light Carmine A	20	Rose	35
Light Carmine, No. 1	20	Superior English Pink	23
Carmine, No. 2	23	Peach Blossom	35
Deep Carmine, No. 3	28	Dubarry Pink	28

Purples

Crimson Purple	63	Purple, No. 2	43
Deep Purple	53	Ruby Purple	73
Crimson Lake	35	Maroon	73
Pansy	43		

Carnations

Carnation, No. 1	20	Carnation	20

Carnation, deep 20

Violets

Deep Violet of Gold	43	Light Violet of Gold	35
Gray Violet of Iron	20	Violet of Iron	28

Ochres

Dark Ochre	20	Yellow Ochre	20

Best Orange 20

Yellows

Ivory Yellow	20	Alberts Yellow	35
Jonquil Yellow	16	Canary Yellow	22
Orange Yellow	16	Silver Yellow	16
Permanent Yellow	16	Yellow for mixing	16
Flux (Foudant Gèneral)	16	(Relief) for Gold	16

Egg Yellow . . . . 28 . . .

Whites

Chinese White 20   Permanent White 16
Relief White (aufsetzweiss) 20

LACROIX'S ENAMEL COLORS.

FOR GROUNDING.

These colors are available for grounds only and will not bear mixing.

Per Tube.		Per Tube.	
Celestial Blue	23	Turquoise Green	28
Indian Blue	28	Steel Grey	20
Lavender Blue	16	Turtle-dove Gray	20
Marine Blue	28	Chinese Yellow	16
Turquoise Blue	28	Isabella	16
Carmelite	16	Fusible Lilac	20
Celadon	20	Maize	20
Shammy Brown	16	Mauve	35
Light Coffee	16	Coral Red	16
Reddish Brown	20	Rose Pompadour	35
Chrome Water Green	16	Salmon	20
Copper Water Green	16	Gold Bud	25
Grounding Green	20	Very Fusible Rose	20

A good precaution in using Tube Colors consists in not laying them back in the box on the same side each time, this will prevent the color from separating from the liquid with which it is mixed. Tube colors should be kept away from heat.

MÜLLER & HENNIG'S

ROYAL DRESDEN CHINA COLORS

In Tubes like Moist Oil or Water for Painting
China, Earthernware, etc.

White

No.	Per Tube	No.	Per Tube
1 Relief White (Aufsetzweiss)			25

Yellows

2 Egg Yellow (Eigelb) 25	35 Ivory Yel .(Elfenbeingelb) . . 25
3 Lemon Yel.(Citronengelb) . 25	41 Albert Yel.(Albertsgelb) . . . 40
4 Canary Yel. (Canariengelb) . 25	45 Yellow Ochre(Ockergelb,) . . 25

5 Relief Yellow (Aufsetzgelb) 25

Greens

6. Yellow Green (Gelbgruen) . 30	12 Olive Gr'n(Olivengruen,) . . 30
7 Blue Green,lt (Blaug'nhell) . 40	25 Grass Green (Glasgruen) . . . 30
8 " dk (" dunkel) . 40	39 Turq'se Gr'n(Turkisgruen,) . . 60
9 Dark Green)Dnukeloruen), . 30	40Black Gr'n (Schwarzgruen) . . ,30

10 Shading Green (Schattirgruen) 30
52 Brown Green 30

Blues

12 Air Blue (Luftblau) 35	15 Turquoise Blue
23 Dark Blne (Dunkelblau,) . 45	(Turkisblau) 55
14 Carm'e Blue (Carminblau,) . 70	26 Light Blue (Hellblau) 30

16 Banding Blue (Raenderblau) 25
56 Delft Blue 25

Pinks and Purples

17 Rose Purple (Resenpurpur) 45
18 Carmine Purple (Carminpur) 65
19 Deep Purple (Dunkelpurpur) 70
30 Deep Violet (Violet dunkel) 70
21 Blue Violet (Blauviolet) 40

54 Ruby Purple 70	38 Rose (Rosa) . . . . . . , . . 40
55 Violet of Iron 25	53 Carmine 50

Reds

22 Yellow Red (Gelbroth) . . . . : 25
23 Pompadour Red (Pompadour) 25
24 Brown Red (Braunroth) 25
34 Flesh Red (Fleischfarbe) 25
44 Pompadou Red, 1st quality (Pompadour 1st quality) 35

Browns

17 Finishing Brown (Ausarbeitungsbraun) 30
28 Sepia Brown (Sepiabraun) 25
29 Yellow Brown (Gelbbraun) 25
30 Dark Brown (Dunkelbraun) 25
36 Chocolate Brown (Chocoldnbn) 30
43 Chestnut Brown (Kastanienbru) 30

Blacks

31 Brunswick Black (Braunschweigerschwarz) 70
32 Outlining Black (Schriftschwarz) 30

Greys

33 Grey for Flowers (Grau fer Blumen) 30
36 Grey for flesh (Grau fer Fleish) 30

Flux

40 Flux (Fluss) 25

Sample Plates

Showing a full line of the above colors fired . . . . each $4.60

MATT OR GOUACHE COLORS

IN POWDER, FINELY GROUND

For Royal Worcester and Doulton Decorations

	Per Bottle.		Per Bottle.
Maroon	.15	Black	.10
Purple	. .15	Celeste Green	10
Pink	10	Emeraid Green .	10
Flesh	.10	Dark Blue	10
Light Yellow	.10	Light Blue . . .	1
Orange	. .10	Dark Brown . . .	10
Light Green	.10	Light Brown . .	. .10
Dark Green	.10	Red Brown . . .	.10
Light Bronze Green . .	.10	Bronze, No. 1	10
Dark Bronze Green	.10	Bronze, No. 2	.10
Light Olive Bronze Green . . .	.10	Red	.10
Dark Olive Bronze Green . . .	.10	Old Rose	10
Chocolate	. .10	Matt Vellum	.10
Ivory	.10	Robin's Egg Blue . .	10
Apple Green	.10	Matt White	.10
Chrome Green		. . . .	.10

INSTRUCTIONS FOR PAINTING WITH MATT COLORS.

What can be done with these colors can be seen on most of the Art Pieces of the Royal Worcester Porcelain Works, when they are used in connection with gold outlining and raised gold work.   The colors are fired the same as Ena mel China Colors (rose color heat) if used on china and earthernware, and the same as glass colors if used on glass but come out of the kiln with no gloss whatever, but a beautiful matt velvety appearance, in fact many of the Gouache Colors look, after they are fired, like unscoured genuine Gold Bronzes. They are mixed the same as ordinary powder colors for overglass painting, with thick oil and turpentine. Unlike other colors for china painting if you want to produce a light tint with any of the Gouache Colors, it is not done by putting a very thin coat on the ware, but by mixing Matt White nto the Gouache Colors and then putting on a coat of the usual thickness. White is used very frequently and Gouache Colors are employed in a similar way to opaque water colors. Very beautiful effects are produced by tracing gold lines on the Gouache Colors.

Gouache Colors are made to be used for artistic purposes, that is for works of art, such as Vases and Placques, and not for general decoration on dinner sets, etc.

MATT OR GOUACHE COLORS

FOR TINTING BACKGROUNDS

In Royal Worcester and Doulton Decoration. Finely ground in Oil, ready for use, in ¼ ounce Bottles.

Price, 15 cents.   By mail, 17 cents per bottle.

Satin Finish	Olive Bronze Green
Matt Vellum for Royal	Light Blue
Worcester ground	Light Brown
Pink	Robin's Egg Blue
Old Rose	Light Green
Flesh	Matt White
Light Yellow	Orange
Ivory	Chrome Green

Apple Green

TINTING IN MATT OR ENAMEL COLORS
PRACTICALLY EXPLAINED.

— —

Mix the color in the bottle thoroughly, and if too thick, add turpentine or Lavender oil and mix well together, put a portion in a saucer, apply a a thin and even coat to the china with a tinting brush, let stand for three minutes, then pad evenly with a pad made by tieing a ball of cotton in either a piece of silk or muslin about six inches square. After the color is perfectly dry Paste for Raised Gold may be worked over it. If flowers are to be painted in the background the tint must be removed with taking out mixture, or it can be scraped out with a knife. All light shades, such as Satin finish, Vellum, Ivory, or White, may be painted over without removing the ground; the background of course must be fired first. Tinting should always be done in a room where there is no carpet on the floor, for if any particles of lint settle on the color before it is dry the lint draws the color around it, and it will show more so after it is fired than before. The color left over in the saucer, can be put back in the bottle, keep well corked and it is ready for the next time. It will keep indefinitely, but do not forget that it is to be mixed thoroughly before use, as the color being heavier than the oil. settles to the bottom, if too thick, add turpentine or lavender oil as stated above. Tinting with my ready mixed Enamel Colors is done in exactly the same way as with Matt Colors. To produce a semi-glaze mix one part of Enamel Color to four parts of Matt Color, Best Rose to Pink, Yellow to Light Yellow, etc.

HALL'S SUPERIOR LIQUID LUSTRES.

— —

15 cents per Bottle.

— —

Ruby	Light Grey
Rose	Pearl Grey
Steel Blue	Yellow
Copper	Dark Green
Silver	Light Green
Brown	Violet
Shammy Brown	Gold Lustre

For directions see next page

Liquid Lustres are generally used for lining the insides of after dinner coffees, or for covering the feet of vases, etc., they are very effective when applied as a background, and a design worked over with raised paste or fine designs in flat gilding, they must of course be fired before the paste or gold is applied. To insure the lustre being even when applied to the china the article must be warmed slightly, and the lustre put on in a thin wash with a flat brush, should the lustre be too thick. thin with essence for liquid bright gold and lustres. Fire to a high degree of heat.

NOTE.—The bottle or vials containing the Lustres are from one-third to three quarters full, according to value of Lustre.

OILS ETC.

—

Turpentine, best ½ pt. bottle, . 15	Lavender oil, ½ oz, bottle, ... 10
Thick or fat oil, ½ oz. " . 10	English Groundlaying oil, ½ oz, bot'10
Tinting Oil, ½ oz. " . 10	Oil of Tar, ½ oz, bottle 10

Balsam of Copaiba 10
Hall's Relief Medium, ½ ounce bottle 15
Hall's Ceramic Fat Oil, ½ ounce bottle 15
Bright Gold Essence, to use with Liquid Bright Gold, Liquid Bright
    Silver and Lustres, ¼ ounce bottle 10
The above oils will be sent by mail at 12 and17 cents per bottle. Turpentine can only be sent by express.

Taking out mixture, 1-2 ounce Jar . . . . · · 10

Taking out mixture is used to erase the design in tinted backgrounds. When the color (ground) has become perfectly dry, sketch the design in with a lead pencil, or trace, then take a small portion of the mixture and place on a palette or slab, add as much oil of lavender (do not use turpentine) to it as there is mixture, mix well together, and with a No. 2 shader fill in the design, applying the mixture in a thin even coat, use a fine tracer for the stems, when the design is covered take a piece of soft rag or cotton and wipe off the mixture the color underneath will come off with it, if it should not wipe up clear, let it stand a few minutes to allow the mixture to soften the color, a piece of cotton slightly made damp with water will afterwards remove all oily substance, wipe very lightly or you are liable to remove or rub the main ground, although there is little or no danger if the ground is perfectly dry.

French Camel Hair Brushes, Etc.
FOR CHINA PAINTING. SUPERIOR QUALITY.

Square Shaders, No. 1 . . each 8
" " " 2 . . " 10
" " " 3 . . " 10
" " " 4 . . " 10
" " " 5 . . " 12
" " " 6 . . " 15
Fitch Stipplers, No. 1 . . " 10
" " " 2 . . " 12
" " " 3 . . " 15
Color Blenders 25
Pointed Shaders' No; 1, . each 7
" " " 2, . " 08
" " " 3. . " 10
" " " 4, . " 10
" " " 5, . " 12
" " " 6, . " 15

Tracers, No. 1, large . . . . each 10
" " 2, medium . . . . " 8
" " 3, small . . . . " 7
*Liners, " 1, large . . . . " 15
" " 2, medium . . . " 12
" " 3, small . . . . " 10
Tinting Brushes, small . . 10 and 15
" " medium, . . each 25
" " large . . . . . " 30
Brushes for spots in gilding . . . 7
Paste Brushes 7
Red Sable Brushes for Relief
   Paste Work and White
   Enamel . . . . No. 1, 15
Red Sable Brushes for Relief
   Paste Work and White
   Enamel . . . . . . No. 2, 20

Glass Brushes, for polishing Gold, large . . . . each, 50
" " " " medium . . . . " 25
" " " " small . . . . " 15
Best Steel Palette Knives, 3 or 3½ inch blades . . . . " 25
Tracing Paper, per sheet 5
Blood Stone Burnishers . . . . each, 60 and 75
Agate Stone Tracers . . . . each, 25
Ground Glass Slabs, 4 x 4 inches . . . . " 5
" " " 6 x 6 " . . . . " 8
" " " 8 x 8 " . . . . " 15
         Ground glass slabs cannot be sent by mail.
Glass Mullers, small . . . . each 10 cents; by mail, 15
" " large . . . . " 20 " " 30
Bone Palette Knives, 5 inch 12

BURNISHING SAND FOR BURNISHING ROMAN GOLD AND BRONZES.

¼ ounce bottle . . . . 10 cents; by mail, 12
½ " . . . . 15 " " 20

*For lining and Banding on a decorators wheel.

BURNISHING SAND.

¼ pound . . . . 75 "   by mail 80
½   "   . . . . 1.35 "   "   1.45
Pound . . . . 2.50 "   "   2.70
Sample Plate of 24 Enamel colors, fired in . . . . each, 50
"   "   30 Matt or Gouache colors, fired in . . . . " 50
"   "   Roman Gold and Bronzes, 10 shades, fired in . . . " 50

Hall's Specially Prepared Relief Enamels.

In Glass Jars.   Price. per Jar, 25 cents.

White Enamel.   Pink (Rose) Enamel
Turquoise "   Coral Red   "

The above Enamels are mixed with an entirely new preparation or medium, they are ground exceedingly fine, and put up in small glass jars, are always ready for use, will not harden while in the jar, but dries in an hour or so when applied to the ware, they will not blister or scale in firing, as is very often the case when mixed with fat oil. Another excellent feature is, that they may be applied to the ware in *high relief*, providing that the color is not used too thin.

INSTRUCTIONS FOR USING THE ENAMELS.

Remove a little of the enamel from the jar to a clean glass slab, if too thick, add a drop or two of clean turpentine and mix well together (a steel palette knife may be used in the mixing process, it will not discolor the enamels), apply to the ware same as paste for raised gold; in relief, it may be worked over any tint or color before firing, without danger of one mixing with the other, providing the tint or color is perfectly dry. For enamel work on gold it is advisable to first fire the gold, and after doing so, and before applying the enamel, polish the gold with a glass brush.   The gold and enamel work may be accomplished at one firing if desired. In this case apply the gold, and when it has become partly dried, scratch out with a knife or brush handle wherever you wish to put the enamel. Fire to a regular gold heat.

Hall's Relief Medium.

In ½ ounce Bottles. Price per Bottle, 15 cents.

To mix with the Relief Colors in powder, such as White Enamel, Turquoise, Pink, Coral Red and Paste for Raised Gold. To two parts of enamel or paste add one part of *Relief Medium*, mix well together with a little turpentine, and apply in relief, Enamels and paste mixed with this *Medium* will not blister or scale in firing.

Jewels and Jewel Cement.

Rubies, Sapphires, Emeralds, Topazes, Turquoises and Crystals, from Nos.
1 to 8. Price, per dozen................. 10
Cut Jewels of the same size and color. Price, per dozen.............20
Cement for fastening jewels, per vial..... 10

Instructions for the Use of Jewels.

Mix the cement with a little thick oil, about same quantity of oil as cement, rather stiff, and apply to the china in dots, where you wish the jewels. Pick up the jewels with a brush handle slightly moistened with thick oil; lay the jewel on the spot of cement and press down slightly.

If you wish to insert the jewels in raised paste, mix one part of cement to two parts of raised paste, or the jewels will not stick properly after firing.

The jewel is placed in the paste for raised gold, pressed down in it and fired together with the paste. The gold is then put on the paste surrounding the jewels at the same time the gilding of the piece is done, and the ware is then fired again. Care must be taken in firing jewels, as too much heat will cause them to flow and lose their shape.

PASTE FOR RAISED GOLD.

Paste for Raised Gold, in powder, per bottle ....,.........10
Paste for Raised Gold in powder, double size 20
Paste for Raised Gold, in powder, per ounce 50
Paste for Raised Gold, per ½ ounce........ 25
Paste for Raised Gold, in glass jar, Ground in Oil, ready for use, ½ oz...25
Paste for Raised Gold, in glass jar, Ground in Oil, ready for use, ounce..50

HOW TO MIX AND APPLY PASTE FOR RAISED GOLD.

To two parts of Paste in powder add one part of Hall's Relief Medium and turpentine sufficient to make a thick paste. Mix well together with a steel palette knife, keep in as small a space on the palette as possible; it will require to be remixed frequently as the turpentine soon evaporates. When doing so add a drop or so of turpentine only. Should it become too fat or oily mix a little more dry color with it.

Use a No. 2 or 3 tracer for fine work, such as lines or spots, and a No. 1 or 2 shader for flowers, leaves, etc.

The brush must never be filled with color, but simply taken up in a ball or knob with the point of the brush; lay the paste as lightly as possible by dragging it from the brush. Never allow the brush to press on the paste in making fine lines. Care must be taken to join the fine lines while the paste is moist.

Relief Enamels and White Enamel should all be mixed and applied the same as Paste for Raised Gold.

CEMENT FOR MENDING CHINA

In Powder, per bottle $0.10
Ready Mixed with oil 0.25

DIRECTIONS FOR MENDING and FIRING CHINA

This cement is a white powder, which is mixed with either water or fat oil, to the consistency of a thick paste. Apply this paste to the broken edges of the ware, press them firmly together and tie with asbestos cord. (The asbestos cord will not injure the color or gold that it may come in contact with in firing). Let the article so mended stand until the cement has become dry, when the pieces will adhere to each other sufficiently well to place the ware in the kiln for firing. Fire the same as decorated articles.
Asbestos cord, per skein. $0.05

MINERAL DECALCOMANIA
FOR BURNING IN ON PORECLAIN, CHINA, WHITEWARE, ETC.

The art of decalcomania has now been successfully before the public for many years. The above is a still later invention, and only recently brought to the market. It has often been remarked and complained about, whether the durability of a transferred article, particularly on china, porcelain or glass, could not be improved upon, therefore after numerous trials and exertions it has been brought as near perfection as possible, thus meeting a demand often made. Articles ornamented in this manner and after going through the regular process of burning in will be found as durable and impossible to deface as the finest hand-painted work.

COMBINATION OF MINERAL DECALCOMANIA.

These designs may be combined to make a very elaborate and hand-
some ornamentation, but they must not be transferred to overlap each
other; the combination must be formed by closely joining the various parts.
If the colors are permitted to overlap they will not fire perfectly.

To those who do not wish to undergo a regular study of china painting the art of transferring mineral Decalcomania to china will be found
very fascinating and simple, also very profitable, for many of the designs,
which cost from 25 to 50 cents, would be worth several dollars if painted by
hand, and these works of art are executed by the best artists of the present
time, therefore it would take years of study to imitate them. For they are
not simply daubs, but equal to the finest paintings executed by hand. They
will also be of great benefit to the artist in helping them to combine one class
of decoration with another.

The price of transfers are from one to fifty cents each, and the sizes vary
from half an inch to eight or ten inches.

The variety (which is very large) consists of figure prices for vases and
centres of plates; cupids, single and double, from one to six inches; flowers
and fruit pieces, groups and single sprays from one to eight inches; roses,
moss and tea, groups and sprays, from one to six inches; figures in groups,
from 2¼ to six inches; butterflies, large and small; landscapes, 3½ by 4½
inches for vases, plates, etc.; roses, small, Dresden style; roses in long
sprays from four to eight inches; birds in group of flowers, for centre of
plates or for vases, 6 by 6, very fine; wild roses, in curved sprays, for side
of plates or vases, very fine; long sprays of mixed flowers for plates; violets
in upright or sprigs, 3 by 4 inches; gene pictures, from one to six inches
square, very fine, for box lids, pin trays, C and B trays, vases, etc.; lilacs,
assorted sizes, very fine; sprays of flowers, very fine, 1½ by 2½ inches; Roman heads, 2½ by 4 inches; female heads, in mandolins, 2 by 3 inches; female
heads, 2 by 2½ inches; animals in ovals, 2 by 3 inches; deers, 3½ by 4
inches; children in squares, single, 3½ by 4½ inches; swans and storks, suitable for 6 by 6 inch tiles; figures, double, 3 by 3½ inches; small sprays of
flowers and blossoms, suitable for trinket sets, A. D., coffees, etc.

HOW TO TRANSFER THE DESIGNS.

Lay the transfer, face upwards, on a damp piece of blotting paper, and
cover with a dry piece. Allow it to remain there for five or ten minutes.
Give the article to which the transfer is to be applied a thin, even coat
of Hall's Transfer Liquid for Mineral Decalcomania (no other form of oil
will answer the purpose), and allow it to dry for five or six minutes. If
the oil or varnish feels tacky and sticks to the finger it is dry enough. Then
lay the transfer on the space to be decorated and cover it with a damp piece
of chamois skin, roll it down with the rubber, proceeding from the centre;

by this process all blisters will easily be removed. The damp chamois makes the paper soft and pliable. The article may be placed in a pail of water, leaving it there until the paper comes off by itself.

Wash the picture with the camel hair brush a little to remove the preparation that is left on from the paper, then lay a piece of damp chamois over the picture and roll it down slightly with rubber roller.

It is not necessary to remove the varnish which will show around the picture, as the same will disappear by the firing process.

Let the article dry for an hour, when it will be ready for firing.

If, after firing, any retouching is needed it can be done with either tube or powder colors.

The transfer liquid being liable to become thick, thus making it difficult to apply sufficiently thin, it is necessary to occasionally reduce same with turpentine.

Parties meeting with difficulty in transferring the designs will please inform me, and I will at once give explanations how to avoid same.

Transfer Liquid for Mineral Decalcomania, ½ ounce bottle...........$0.15
Rubber Rollers ....each .35
Flat Brush to apply Liquid...............................each .15
Round Brush to Wash Pictures............................each .15

I will send a sample of two dozen pictures, assorted sizes and designs (my own selection); rubber roller, ½ ounce bottle of transfer liquid and two brushes for $2.00, postage paid.

By mentioning the articles you wish to decorate I will send, as near as possible, appropriate designs for same.

⇒≡ PRICE LIST ≡⇐

OF

Mineral ⚜ Decalcomanie

For Burning in on Porcelain, China, White Ware, etc.

No.				Size by Inches.		Price
1. Small single Cupids, very fine				¾x1½	each	08
2. " double "		"		1½x1½	"	10
3. Large single "		"		1½x1½	"	15
4. " double "		"		4x4	"	50
5. " " "		"		2x2	"	15
6. " " "		"		2½x2½	"	20
7. " " "		"		3x3	"	30
8. Genre Pictures, very fine				2½x2½	"	25
9. Genre Pictures, "				3x3	"	35
10. Small Flowers, assorted, very fine					"	1, 2, 3
11. Children's Heads in Flowers, Baskets of Flowers, Horse Shoes, etc., very fine,				1½ to 3	"	5 to 10
12. Landscapes in Flower Sprays "				2½x3½	"	25

13. Swans and Storks . . . . 5x6 . . . each 25
14. Flower Pieces for centre of plates . . . . 4x4 . . . " 25
15. Sprays of Violets, assorted, per sheet . . . . " 25
16. American Fishes, very beautiful . . . . . 2½x5½ . . . " 30
17. " " . . . . 1¼x3 . . . " 10
18. Animal Heads, ... 2¼x3 . . . " 04
19. Landscapes and Marine Views . . . . . . 3x5 . . . " 10
20. Landscapes in flower designs . . . . . . 4x4 . . . " 15
21. Animals, Deer, Horses, Bears, etc . . . . 3 to 4 . . . " 10 and 15
22. Children in Squares . . . . 3½x4½ . . . " 15
23. Chinese Figures . . . . 4x6 . . . " 25
24. Double Cupids . . . . 3x5 . . . " 10
25. Children Scenes, Greenway style . . . . 5¼x1½ . . . " 35
26. Small Flowers, assorted styles and designs, ¾x1¼ . . . " 01
27. " " 1 to 2 . . . " 02
28. " " " 1½ to 2½ . . . " 03
29. " " " 2 to 3¼ . . . " 04
30. Flower Spreys, assorted, very fine . . . . 1¾x3 . . . " 05
31. Birds, Bees, Bugs, Birds in Landscapes, etc. . . . . . . " 1 to 5
32. Butterflies, all varieties and sizes . . . . " 1 to 5
33. Game Set, Birds in Branches, 20 pieces, Frogs, etc ,
   very fine, ... 7x7 . . . per set, 5.00
34. Game Set, in natural colors, very fine . . . 4x5 per set of 12, 2.50
35. " Birds and Landscapes, " . . . 2x3½ set, 1.50
36. " In natural colors . . . . 2¾x4½ . . . " 1.50
37. " very good . . . . 2¼x4 . . . " 2.25
38 Birds on branches and in landscapes, very fine, 2½x4 each, 10 to 25
39. " " ' " " 2x5½ " 20
40. Birds and Flowers very fine . . . . 2x4 " 15
41. Birds and Landscapes, assorted . . . . . . ¾x1¼ " 05
42. Female Figure and Child, 2 different, very
   fine, for plaques and vases . . . . . . 5½x8 " 60
43. Male and Female, single figures for vases,
   etc., very fine . . . . 3x5 " 35
44. Female Figures for vases . . . . 3x5 " 25
45. Genre Pictures for plaques or plates . . . 6x6 " 75
46. Genre" " " . . . 5x5 " 50
47. Faust and Marguerite . . . . 3¾x4¾ " 25
48. Double Figures, Dancing Girls, etc.. . . . 3½x5 " 25
49. " " " " . . . 2½x3½ " 20
50. " " Children Scenes . . . 2x4 " 15
51. " " " " . . . . 3x4 " 25
52. " " Wattean style . . . . . 2¼x3¼ " 15
53. Figure Groups, Rococco style . . . . . . 2x3 " 20
54 Children Scenes, Rococco style . . . . . 2½x3 " 20
55. " " " 2½x4 " 20
56. Figure Pieces, Watteau style . . . . . . 2½x2½ " 10
57. Illustrations of well known Fables . . . . 3¼x4½ " 25
58. " " " . . . 2¼x3¼ " 15
59· Cupids in Groups, 12 in set . . . . . . per set, 3,70

60.	Large Single Cupids, very fine	4x5	each,	30
61.	Single Cupids '	3x3	"	20
62.	" "	2½x3¼	"	25
63.	" "	1¼x1¾	"	08
64.	" "	¾x1¾	"	06
65.	" "	2¼x2⅓	"	15
66,	Fruit Pieces, for fruit sets	4½x4½	"	40
67.	" " "	3½x3½	"	25
68.	Sprays of Honeysuckles, assorted sizes, very fine	2½ to 7	"	10, 15, 20
69.	Flower Sprays, assorted, very fine	4x8	"	25
70.	" " "	3½x7	"	20
71.	" " "	2x4½	"	10
72.	" " very delicate	2½x6	"	20
73.	Pink and Blue Flower Sprays, very good	2¼x5	"	10
74.	Sprays of Forget-me-nots, very fine	2¼x2½	"	10
75.	" Wild Roses, very fine, assorted		"	1 to 20
76.	" " "	1 to 5	"	1 to 15
77.	" " "	1 to 6	"	1 to 15
78.	Dresden Flower Sprays	1 to 6	"	1 to 15
79.	Flower Groups, assorted	4½x6	"	20
80.	Pink and Blue Flower Sprays	4x5	"	06
81.	English Holly Sprays	1½ to 6	"	2 to 15
82.	Flower Sprays in Pink and Green very delicate and fine	1 to 6	"	1 to 15
83.	Flower Groups, for plates, assorted very fine	1½ to 6½	"	2 to 25
84.	Sprays of Blue Flowers, assorted	4½x6	"	10 to 20
85.	Female Heads	4¼x5½	"	50
86.	"	3x5	"	35
87.	" very fine	2¼x3½	"	25
88.	" "	1½x2½	"	05
89.	" "	1½x2	"	15
90.	" in medalion	1½x2	"	05
91.	"	¾x1¼	"	03
92.	" in round medalions	1¼x1¼	"	03
93.	Heads of Kings and Queens, very fine	2½x7½	"	20
94.	Children's Heads "	1¾x2¾	"	05
95.	Queens' Heads "	1x1	"	10
96.	Conventional Designs, of flowers in grey and orange, very good	1 to 6½	"	1 to 20
97.	Thistle Sprays	3x7	"	25
98.	Assorted Flowers, in groups, good	3¼x3½	"	25
99.	" " "	3½x4½	"	25
100.	Sprays of Roses, Poppies, etc., very fine	5½ to 6	"	15
101.	Flower Sprays, assorted	3¼x4½	"	12
102.	" "	2¼x4½	"	08
103.	" "	3¼x4½	"	10
104.	Flower pieces, suitable for Brush and Comb trays, Pansys, Azaleas, and Anemones, very delicate in color.	4x6	"	20

NOTE.—When ordering Decalcomania, please order by number only.

HALL' GOLD AND COLOR ERASER

This eraser is used to remove gold or color from china that has been fired in. It contains no hydrofluric acid, therefore wil not burn or injure the hands or clothing. It is a useful article, and a bottle should always be kept handy in the studio, for very often a spot of gold or color is discovered on a very handsomely decorated piece of china after firing, which is an eyesore to most every one. This can very readily be removed by simply applying a spot of this Eraser with an old brush or match stick, and allowing it to stand for a few seconds, then wipe off with a wet sponge or cloth.

It may also be used for engraving on glass with either brush or pen work. Any ordinary pen will answer the purpose. Be sure and mix the Eraser well in the bottle before using, by either shaking or stirring, and use from the bottle only. Price per bottle, 25 cents.

BARGAIN LIST, No. 2
...OF...

⇒⊁Enamel · Powder › Colors⊀⇐

FINELY GROUND AND FLUXED

Mix with a little Thick Oil and Turpentine.   **For Full Directions See Page 19 of Catalogue.**

These colors are equal in every respect to the regular Enamel Colors, but are not catalogued. There are from fifty to two hundred bottles of each color. Therefore, when ordering, please mention a second choice; first choice will in all cases be sent while stock is complete. Give number of color only. The price is 5 cents per bottle, except Nos. 3 and 13, which are 10 cents per bottle, postpaid.

No.
1 No. 2 Blue (rich shade like Indigo).
2 Steel Gray (very light, fine for ground laying).
3 Crimson (very rich, similar to Deep Purple).
4 Carmine (Dark similar to Japan Rose but deeper).
5 Pink (like English Rose color, good for Pink roses).
6 Best Red (Poppy color).
7 Coral Red (Yellowish).
8 No. 3 Turquoise (green shade)
9 Purple Brown (a deep Chocolate).
10 Crest Brown (similar to Turtle Dove Gray, but darker).
11 Lustre Brown (similar to Yellow Brown.)

12 No. 1 Fawn (yellowish tint, for grounds).
13 No. 3 Blue (the nearest shade to underglaze Blue, for painting, tinting or ground laying; the darkest enamel Blue Made).
14 Buff (like Yellow Brown).
15 Lavender (for grounds or tinting).
16 Light Brown (similar to Light Brown, regular colors).
17 Laque (a Light Violet, good for painting or tinting).
18 Sap Green (similar to La Croix Brown Green, but lighter).
19 Gray (very dark, good for tinting or painting).
20 Brown Green (greener shade than No. 18).
21 Egg Yellow (very rich).
22 Deep Chrome Green (like La Croix Deep Chrome Green).
23 Primrose (a very light yellow for tinting).
24 Turquoise Green (for grounds, very rich).
25 Blue Green (Turquoise shade, excellent for grounds).
26 Matt Dark Blue Green (very rich).
27 No. 4 Turquoise (like Water Green, for grounds).
28 Vert-de-eau (a beautiful Water Green, for grounds).
29 Orange (darker shade than regular Orange).
30 Yellow Green (shade lighter than Apple Green).
31 Turquoise (for ground laying, like No. 25, but lighter).
32 Paste (for Liquid Bright Gold and Liquid Lustres).
33 Yellow (similar to Mixing Yellow).
34 Brilliant Black (very good, only 25 bottles in stock).
35 Light Brown (for painting, like Brown No. 4 or 7
36 Sepia (one of the richest colors on the list, darker than Brown 4 or 17).
37 No. 4 Green (similar to Green 36—T, very good for painting).
38 No. 3 Brown (like Brown M or 108).
39 Matt Dark Brown (very rich).

When ordering above colors, please give number only.

Price List for Firing and Gilding China.

We fire every working day in the year. China left to be fired before 2 P. M. will be ready for delivery on and after 8 A. M. the following day. We make a specialty of firing china, and have four of the finest kilns in the country. Special firing done at a nominal extra cost, viz.: If a few pieces of china are left at 2 P. M. they will be fired and ready for delivery at 5.30 P. M. same day. The charges will be double regular rates. We also make a specialty of artistic gilding at very low rates. Tinting, groundlaying and painting done to order in the latest styles and at a few hours' notice.

Hard Kiln Firing

We fire a hard kiln on the first Monday in every month. China groundlaid in hard kiln colors to order, and at reasonable rates. Hard kiln firing is done by no other house in the country. The colors mostly admired in hard kiln grounds are ruby, maroon, amber, Rose du Barry, pinks, golden fawn, greens and celadous. Parties at a distance can have any article of china groundlaid and fired hard kiln by sending rough sketch of design and stating what shade of color they desire. The price of groundlaying and firing hard kiln are double regular rates. For instance, a $7\frac{1}{2}$-inch plate groundlaid, 1 or 2-inch band, and fired, would cost 50 cents. Other shapes and sizes accordingly. All orders for above work must be in at least one week before day of firing. White china furnished at regular retail prices. No charge is made for packing.

Every possible care is guaranteed, and I hold myself responsible for china that should happen to break in firing. China sent by express will receive prompt attention, and will be fired same day as received and returned carefully packed by an experienced packer the day following. No charge will be made for repacking.

	FIRING.		GILDING. [Edges only	
	Each	Dozen	Each	Doz.
Tea Cups and Saucers, 2 pcs.	10	1.00	10	$1.00
Small Coffee and Saucer, "	10	1.00	10	1.00
Large " " "	10	1.00	10	1.00
After Dinner" ," "	08	75	08	75
Mustache Cup and Saucer, "	12		10	
Individual Butters	3	30	3	30
Tea Pots 10, 15, 20			10	
Sugar Bowl, large	15		10	
" small	10		8	
Sugar Box with lid, large · .	20		10	
" " small . .	10		8	
Cream Pitchers 5, 8, 10			5, 10	

	Each	Dozen	Each	Dozen
Cake or Bread Plates	10, 12		10, 12	
Egg Cups	03	3 !	03	30
Candlesticks	5, 8, 10		5, 08	
Pitchers, half pint	06		08	
" pint	12		10	
" quart	15		12	
" 3-pint	20		15	
" half gallon	25		20	
" gallon	35		25	
Vases, 4 inches high	05		05	
" 5 or 6 "	8, 10		08	
" 7 or 8 "	12, 15		10	
" 9 or 10 "	18, 20		12	
" 11 or 12 "	25 30		15	
" 13 or 14 "	35, 40		20	
" 15 or 16 "	45, 50		25	
" 17 or 18 "	55, 60		30	
" 19 or 20 "	75 to 100		35	
" 21 or 22 "	1.00–125		50	
Soup Tureen	35		20	
Sauce Tureen	20		15	
Sauce or Gravy Boat	10		10	
Covered Vegetable Dish, oval	30		25	
" " round,	25		20	
Salad Bowls	15, 20		10, 12	
Olive Dishes	05		05	
Baskets	8, 10, 12, 15		8, 10	
Pickle Dishes	7, 8		5	
Comports	10, 15, 20		10, 15	
Butter Dish with lid	15, 20		15	
Ice Cream Saucers	5	50	5	50
Ice Cream Dish	15, 20, 25		15 to 25	
Ice Cream Plates	6, 7, 8	60 to 75	6, 7	60 to 75
Tete-a-tete Sets	45, 60		25 to 50	
Cuff Buttons, per pair	5	50	5	50
Shaving Cups	8, 10		5, 8	
Chamber Sets, 10 pieces	1.50		1.50	
Chamber Sets, 12 pieces	2.25		2.25	
Tall Coffee and Saucer	8, 10		8, 10	
Bon Bon Box, 2½ inches	5	3 gold lines	10	
Bon Bon Box, 3 inches	8	3 gold lines	12	
Bon Bon Box, 3½, 4 inch	10	3 gold lines	12	
Bon Bon Box, 4½ inches	12	3 gold lines	15	
Bon Bon Box, 5½ inches	15	3 gold lines	20	
Bon Bon Box, 6 inches	20	3 gold lines	25	
Bon Bon Box, 7 inches	25	3 gold lines	25	
Bon Bon Box, 8 inches	28	3 gold lines	30	
Loving Cups	10, 15, 20		8, 10	
Candy Boxes	10, 15, 20	2 lines	15	
Pin Trays	4, 5		5	
Ash Receivers	4, 5		5	

Bone Dishes	5	50	5	50
Jardinier s	20 to 40		
Ring Stand, or Tree.....	5	50	5	50
Cracker Jar, Stand & Lid.	20 to 28	3 lines	15
Rose Jar	10, 15, 20		8 to 15
Marmalade Jar, with Lid and Stand	15 20	3 lines	15
Pen Trays	5, 6, 7		5, 6
Comb and Brush Trays..	10, 12, 15		10, 12
Olive Dishes	5 to 8		5 to 8
Candlesticks, low	5 to 12		3 to 8
Candlesticks, high	10 to 15		8 to 10
Potpourri Jar	10 to 15		8 to 10
Cream Pitchers	7, 8, 10		7 to 10
Chocolate Pots	15 to 25		10, 12
Small Tea Pot, Sugar & Cream	35		25
Manicure Sets, 7 pieces..	25	7 lines	25
Punch Bowl, 12 inches..	40	3 bands	40
Punch Bowl, 14 inches..	50	3 bands	50
Punch Bowl, 16 inches..	75	3 bands	60
Bread & Milk Set, 3 pcs..	25	3 edges	20
Oyster Plates	8, 10	75, 1.00	6, 8	70, 85
Milk Cups	8		5
Individual Salts	3	30	3	30
Pepper Castor	5	2 lines	5
Toilet Sets, 4 pieces.....	28	4 lines	25
Cake Basket, with handle.	20, 25		15
Smoking Set, 6 & 8 pcs..	35 to 50		25 to 35
Clocks	10 to 50		
Pen and Ink Stands.....	10 to 20		15, 20
Lamps	25 to 40		

PLATES.

Firing.
Size in inches........................... 5, 6, 7, 7½, 8 9
Each 05, 06, 07, 08, 10, 10
Dozen 40, 50, 60, 70, 80, 1.00
Gold Edge.
Each 05, 06, 07, 08, 10, 10
Dozen 40, 50, 60, 70, 80, 1.00
Gold Stippled Edge, Rich.
Each 15, 20, 25, 35, 40, 45
Gold Stippled Edge, Slight.
Each 10, 10, 15, 20, 25, 25
Gold Dentelle Edge.
Each 15, 20, 20, 25, 25, 30
Tinted, 1 to 2 inch Band.
Each 10, 12, 15, 15, 20, 25
Dozen 75, 80, 1.25, 1.25, 1.75, 2.00

PLAQUES.

Firing.
Size in inches.................. 10, 11, 12, 12½, 13, 14, 16, 18
Each 12, 15, 15, 18, 20, 25, 30, 40

Gold Edge.
Each. 12, 15, 15,   18, 20, 25, 30, 40
DISHES.
Firing.
Size in inches..................... . 8, 10, 12, 14, 16, 18, 20. 22. 24
Each 10, 10, 12, 15, 20, 25, 30, 40, 50
Gold Edge.
Each 10, 10, 12, 15, 15, 20, 25, 30, 35
TILES.
Firing.
Size in inches........................... .... 3x3, 3x6, 4x4, 6x6, 8x8
Each 03, 05, 05, 08. 10
Dozen 35, 50, 50, 75, 1.00
PANELS.
Firing.
Size in inches.................. 2x2, 3x4, 4x8, 6x8, 8x10, 8x12, 10x15
Each 03, 05, 08, 10. 15   20,   30
                                    Gilt Slight. Gilt Solid.
GILDING HANDLES, ETC.
A. D. Coffee Cup Handle......................   05   10
Pitcher Handles 5, 10, 15, 15, 20, 25, 30
Basket Handles, each................... .... 5, 10, 15, 15, 20, 25, 30
Cake or Bread Plate Handles, each..... ....   10, 15   15,20
Vase Handles, each...................... ....   5 to 20   10 to 50
Tea Pot Handles, each................... ....   5 to 25   10 to 50
Sugar Box Handles, each................. ....   5 to 15   10 to 30
Soup Tureen Handles, each............... ...   10 to 15   25 to 40
Vegetable Dish Handles, each.............. ....   10 to 15   25 to 40
Sauce Tureen Handles, each.......... ....   10 to 15   20 to 30
Gravy Boat Handles, each................ ....   5 to 10   15 to 25
Candy Box Handles, each................. ....   5 to 15   15 to 25
Cream Pitcher Handles, each.............. ....   5 to 10   15 to 25
Loving Cup Handles, each................ ....   10 to 25   15 to 30
GOLD STIPPLED EDGES.
                                                            Each.
Cup and Saucer, any size...............   25
Individual Butters and Salts............. .... 5 to   10
Pitchers and Creams................... .. .. 10 to   25
Vases .... 5 to   25
Ice Cream Saucers..................... .... 5 to   10
Ice Cream Plates...................... .... 10 to   20
Plates .... 10 to   25
Comb and Brush Trays................. .... 20 to   35
Bon Bon Boxes....................... .... 25 to 1.00
Powder Boxes .... 20 to   40
Cracker Jar, with lid and stand........... .... 25 to   50
Plaques .... 15 to   75
Jardinieres .... 25 to 1.00
Dishes .... 15 to 1.00
Loving Cups .... 10 to   25
Candlesticks .... 10 to   25
Bureau Set, 8 to 10 pieces............. .... 75 to 1.00
Smoking Sets, 8 to 10 pieces............. .... 75 to 1.00
    Note.—This Price List is subject to change.